The Force of Joy

by
Jerry Savelle

The Force of Joy

by
Jerry Savelle

Harrison House
Tulsa, Oklahoma

Unless otherwise indicated, all Scripture
quotations are taken from the *King James
Version* of the Bible.

The Force of Joy
ISBN 0-89274-348-4
Copyright © 1988 by Jerry Savelle
P. O. Box 2228
Fort Worth, Texas 76113

Published by Harrison House, Inc.
P. O. Box 35035
Tulsa, Oklahoma 74153

Contents

1
The Forces of Life

My son, attend to my words; incline thine ear unto my sayings.

Let them not depart from thine eyes; keep them in the midst of thine heart.

For they are life unto those that find them, and health to all their flesh.

Keep thy heart with all diligence; for out of it are the issues of life.

Proverbs 4:20-23

One meaning or rendering of verse 23 of this passage is: **Protect your spirit, for out of it are the forces of life.**

God has placed within the reborn human spirit certain forces which He has specifically designed to work efficiently to produce great results. These forces are given to provide everything needed for successful Christian living.

Today many Christians are crying out to God for this or that spiritual "gift":

"Oh, Lord, give me power." "Oh, God, give me love." "Oh, Father, give me faith." They do not realize that God has already put all of these things within their reborn spirits.

As Christians, we have been equipped with all of these forces. The problem is that many believers just let them lie dormant. Such people are like the man who had a million dollars in the bank but who never learned how to write a check. Although a millionaire, that man lived his whole life in poverty because he was not able to take advantage of his resources.

Some Christians pray and beg the Lord, "Oh, God, give me more love!" God can't give any Christian more love than he already has. The Apostle Paul tells us: **....the love of God is shed abroad in our hearts by the Holy Ghost which is given unto us.** God has filled us with Himself. God is love, and we are full of Him. He is on the inside of us. He's as close to us as our next breath. People who beg God for more love are simply ignorant of the fact that they are already filled to overflowing with love—God's love. They already have the answer to their prayer. They are just letting it lie dormant—because of ignorance.

Then there are those people who cry out: "God, give me more faith. Oh, Lord, if I just had more faith!"

Once again, Paul tells us that **....God hath dealt to every man the measure of faith** (Rom. 12:3). This faith is the God-kind of faith. (Mark 11:22.) As Christians we have faith. We received it the moment we were born again. But the problem is, a lot of people have never tapped into the faith they already possess.

Solomon says that we are to protect our spirits, to keep our hearts **with all diligence** (Prov. 4:23). "With all diligence" doesn't mean sloppily. It doesn't mean to be a spiritual sluggard. Solomon didn't tell us to be lazy Christians.

Tapping Your Potential

In the number of years I have been in the ministry, as I have traveled from one end of the country to the other, I have discovered that there are a lot of lazy

Christians in our land. As a result of their laziness, many of these people are "losers" in life. They seem to be upset with those of us who are winning. They are mad at us who succeed, those who are blessed of God. They are jealous, bitter and angry. Why? These people have the same potential as any of the rest of us. The only difference between them and us is the fact that we have tapped into our potential—and they haven't.

One day I had the opportunity to sit down and watch the Super Bowl on television. I don't remember what year it was, but Dallas and Pittsburgh were playing for the championship. As I was sitting there watching the football game and enjoying myself, all of a sudden I heard something come up out of my spirit.

Now I am not a novice at these things, I know the Spirit of God when I hear Him. I distinctly heard the Spirit of the Lord say to me: "Jerry, how many Terry Bradshaws, Franko Harrises, Roger Staubachs, and Tony Dorcettes do you suppose are sitting in their living rooms right now watching these men play?"

Well, the first thing that thrilled me was the realization that God was watching the game. (It is not too often that God speaks to a person while he's watching T.V. In fact, the biggest revelation I've ever received from the Lord while watching T.V. was "Turn it off!")

At first I didn't catch the meaning of what the Spirit had said to me. I was still shocked about God's watching the ball game. I knew He had to be watching because He knew who was playing!

So I said, "Excuse me. Say that again, Lord."

"How many Terry Bradshaws, Franko Harrises, Roger Staubachs and Tony Dorcettes do you suppose are sitting in their living rooms right now watching these men play?"

Then I began to catch the meaning of God's question.

"Son, there are many men sitting in their living rooms with the same potential as those fellows out on that field," He explained. "The 'superstars,' those who are household names — whatever their field or profession — are numerous, but there are many more potential 'superstars' you never hear about because they spend their lives sitting on the sidelines watching someone else play the game for them."

"Son," He confided in me, "there are a great number of men who could be accomplishing the same things as these players. They could become great athletes. They have the same potential as these men have. The only difference between the men on the field and those watching T.V. is that the ones on the field have tapped into their potential — those in front of the T.V. have not."

I realized how true that statement is. We are all given tremendous potential for good in life. Yet so many of us never tap into that potential. How does a person go about doing that? How do you reach down on the inside of yourself and grab ahold of some of that potential and bring it out where you can use it?

My youngest daughter has been taking piano lessons for a number of years. For a long time now her music teacher has been telling her mother and me, "Your daughter has great potential." Every time I hear that statement I always think to myself, "Yes, but how do we tap into it?" Then I realized that we already were doing that.

Have you ever been told that you have potential? Do you know how to tap into the potential you have? If you are a Christian, I can assure you that you do have potential — God-given potential. You have the potential to be a successful person, a winner in life. That is good. It's fun to be a winner with God.

But unfortunately, many Christians, even some ministers, don't know how to tap into their God-given potential. Let me share with you how to do that.

Diligence: Key to Success

Notice in Proverbs 4:23 that Solomon, the wisest man who ever lived, says to protect your spirit. In Proverbs 20:27 this same wise Solomon tells us: **The spirit of man is the candle of the Lord....** You have within your being a spark of the Divine.

Within your spirit (your heart) is the potential to win. The *King James Version* of Proverbs 4:23 says: **Keep thy heart with all diligence....** Diligence is an important word. Many people don't like it because it means work. That is the reason a lot of folks don't like the message of faith. Because it's not a "you-just-sit-there-on-the-bench" message. Faith demands that we get up off the bench and get into the game. Faith requires that we *do* something.

Someone once said to me, "But I thought faith meant that we don't have to work any more."

No, my Bible says, "Faith worketh." (Gal. 5:6.) You will never work so hard in all your life as you will once you start living by faith!

James tells us that **...faith, if it hath not works, is dead....**(James 2:17). And work, in any form of the word, is not a very popular activity. But it is a very rewarding one.

"Protect your spirit with all diligence," the Bible tells us, "for out of it flow the forces of life." These forces of life are the very forces that create and provide for us the kind of life God has ordained for us to live.

Some folks seem to have the mistaken idea that God has ordained for His children to "win a few, lose a few." That God has prearranged our lives to be full of tragedy and woe. That hardship and failure are just God's way of reaffirming His sovereignty, of reminding us that He is still God. That He is still in charge. Some ministers preach that it is not God's will that His children win all the time because if we did we might get the "big head." That is ridiculous. The person who preaches that message is the one with the "big head" — it is swelled up with ignorance!

God wants His children to be winners in life just as much as we want our children to be winners. But in order to live a successful life, you are going to have to learn how to tap into these forces of life. You must learn to be diligent. You can't be sloppy or lazy and win victories. In order to win, you must learn and practice *self*-discipline. This is one thing that no one else can do for you — not even God.

Some people want to be winners. They would like to be successful. But they just don't want to put out what it takes to achieve that success. It's easier to just "take it as it comes." They just figure, "Whatever happens, happens. If it's good, that's great. If it's not, then God's will be done." It's always easier to lay failure off on God than it is to face it and determine to get back up and *do* something about it!

No one becomes a winner in life by just lying down and taking whatever comes. Success demands determination. Winning requires diligence.

It takes a lot of diligence, for example, to become a super athlete.

Once, I had the privilege of preaching to the Chicago Bears professional football team. Some members of that team are turned on to the Word of God. I began talking to that team about developing a winning image. They came alive and began playing better than they had in months.

I asked some of the individual players, "How did you get to be such a great football player?" The answer was obvious. A lot of hard work, a lot of self-discipline, a lot of diligence. While everybody else is doing something a lot more comfortable, those fellows are out on that practice field sweating and straining, getting their minds and bodies into top-notch condition. They can't afford to "take it easy." They know that in order to win, they've got to "give it all they've got," every minute of every day.

That same principle applies to us as Christians. When everyone else is just fooling around and "playing church," we must be out there reading the Word, meditating the Word, confessing the Word, *doing* the Word. James tells us: **But be ye doers of the word, and not hearers only, deceiving your own selves** (James 1:22).

Sometimes that is not the most appealing or the most comfortable thing to do at the moment, especially when you look around you and everyone else seems to be taking life easy. Here you are standing on the Word of God and gritting your teeth and demanding your best, while the world just seems to be gliding along effortlessly. You are holding on for all you're worth, telling yourself, "I don't care how bad it looks, I am not going to quit! I am not going to compromise!" While everyone else is out on the golf course or playing badminton. That is hard. There's no doubt about it, it's rough.

But then when game day comes, guess who wins? Not the golfers or the badminton players. Not the guy who's been lying out on the beach getting a tan. When game day comes, the one who wins is not the one who was in the locker room playing cards. It's the one who was out on the field sweating and straining and working.

When the coach needs somebody with the potential to win the big game, he's not going to pick the card player, nor the suntan artist, nor the "easy-does-it" type. He's going to pick the guy who has taken his natural potential and tapped into it to become a true champion. Through diligence.

A winner is not just the guy who's "got the goods." It's the guy who knows how to take the goods he's got and use them to get the job done.

To be a winner in life, you have got to work at it. You have to learn to get up one more time than you fall down. You have to make up your mind that, come what may, you are not going to give up, you are determined not to be the devil's doormat. You must make up your mind that the enemy is not going to put that sickness in you. You are not going to go broke. You are not going to allow Satan to steal and kill and rob you of your life.

To be a winner in the Christian life, sooner or later you have to set your face like flint, put your faith where your mouth is, and say: "In the Name of Jesus, I don't care what it looks like, devil, I am not going to fail! Because I am going to lay hold onto *the forces of life!*"

2
Source of the Force

But the fruit of the Spirit is love, joy, peace, longsuffering, gentleness, goodness, faith,

Meekness, temperance: against such there is no law.

Galatians 5:22,23

Where this passage says "fruit," insert the word "forces." That will put a whole new perspective on these verses.

Notice that the word "Spirit" in verse 22 is capitalized. In most cases, in the *King James Version* when the word "Spirit" is capitalized, it indicates that the writer was referring to God's Holy Spirit. But that capitalization was not present in the original texts, it was added later at the discretion of the English translators. If you read this whole book of Galatians, you will find that the Apostle Paul was not referring to the Holy Spirit at all here. Rather he was talking about the *reborn* human spirit. The reborn human spirit, through the work of the Holy Spirit, can succeed.

Now I don't want to give the impression that the Holy Spirit is not involved in this spiritual empowering. But it should be obvious by now that not every person who is filled with the Holy Spirit is winning in life. Being filled with God's Spirit does not, of itself, automatically transform an individual into an instant winner. I personally know of many people who have been filled with the Holy Ghost for years, who can talk in tongues with the best of them, yet who are still living fruitless and defeated lives.

That cannot be the fault of God's Holy Spirit. Nor does it necessarily indicate that these people are not Spirit-filled. The problem is not with the Spirit, but with the spirit — their spirit. They have not learned how to tap into the power that is resident within them.

You see, if this fruit were just the work of the Holy Spirit, something that God produced in us on His own, then we would all be winning all the time. But these qualities are not the fruit of God's *Holy* Spirit, rather they are the fruit of the reborn *human* spirit.

These attributes of God were placed in us by His Spirit at the time of the New Birth. In fact, if you will look at the last verse of the book of Galatians, you will see that Paul says to us: **Brethren, the grace of our Lord Jesus Christ be with your spirit** (Gal. 6:18).

What Paul is talking about in this entire last chapter of Galatians is our individual human spirit. Like Solomon of old, Paul is saying to us, "Protect your spirit, for out of it flow the forces of life: love, joy, peace, longsuffering, gentleness, goodness, faith, meekness and temperance."

Love is a *force.* The Bible says that love never fails. (1 Cor. 13:8.) When we walk in the love of God, we are winners, because love never fails. When we are injured, our human flesh may want to retaliate in kind. But if we allow the force of love to flow out from us, it will **overcome evil with good** (Rom. 12:21).

Although everything in life may seem to prove the contrary, when all is said and done, the person who walks in love is going to be the one to come out the winner. Every time.

Love is not just a fruit. It is a tremendous force. It is one of the forces of life. And that love is dwelling in you. You don't need to pray for it any more. It's already there in your spirit. All you need to do is learn how to tap into it.

Joy is another force that resides in your spirit. You may walk around all day long with a frown on your face. That does not mean that joy is not in your spirit. It just means that you've suppressed it. You haven't tapped into it.

Appropriating the joy of the Lord is a matter of choice, an act of the will. You can get up in the morning and *will* to be happy. Or you can *will* to be unhappy. The choice is yours.

When someone says or does something to offend you, you can choose your reaction — either love or hate. But in order to walk in love, in the joy of the

Lord, you will have to reach down into that spirit and tap into the force of life which you need.

Nobody can make you get into strife, not even the devil. The decision to do that resides in your will. Satan can't *make* you do anything. He isn't big enough to force you to do anything against your own free will. All he can do is to try his best to deceive you. Then once you are deceived, by an act of your own will you will choose his way. If you can't be deceived, you won't choose the way of the adversary. If you recognize Satan's deception when it comes, then you have the power to tap into the forces of life within you and walk in victory over him.

This is true in every area of life. It really doesn't matter what kind of obstacle or barrier Satan throws up before you. If you will make up your mind that you are going to tap into whatever force of life is needed in that particular area, you will come out the winner. That force of life will get you over the obstacle and carry you to victory.

Notice that Paul says that love is a force. Joy is a force. Peace is a force. Longsuffering is a force of life.

Longsuffering is so powerful. God is *longsuffering*. If He weren't, He would have given up on us a long time ago. We've "blown it" so many times. But God is longsuffering. The Bible says He is the God of patience. (Rom. 15:5.) He must be to have put up with us all this time.

As weak and prone to failure as we human beings are, we live by faith. So does God. He has to have just as much faith in us as we do in Him. More, in fact. Because God has to place His faith in a frail, human vessel, while we place ours in a Supreme Supernatural Being who cannot fail!

Some people say things like this: "Oh, if God only knew how mean my husband treats me!" "If the Lord only knew how awful my wife acts!" "If He only knew how unfaithful my mate is!"

Have you ever thought about how mean and awful and unfaithful the Bride of Christ has been to Him through the centuries? Yet the Lord has looked beyond all that. He is not moved by what He sees or hears. Nothing we or anyone else can say or do can force Him to change His confession. He says that He is coming back one day for a **glorious church** (Eph. 5:27)!

But look how far short of "glorious" the individual members of that Church fall! Yet God continues to be faithful to His Bride. And to have faith in *our* faithfulness to Him.

Faithfulness, longsuffering, patience — these are some of the forces of God's Spirit. They are a part of His divine nature.

As Christians, we have God's nature in us. If God is a God of patience, then Jerry Savelle is a man of patience. I have the potential to be just as patient as my heavenly Father. I have the potential to love as God loves, to be just as strong in faith as God is, because it is the God-kind of faith that I possess.

All of the forces of God are in me. If you are a believer, they are also in *you*. God Himself put them there by His Spirit.

Developing Life Forces

None of these forces of life works automatically. They must be released by the person who possesses and controls them. Faith, meekness, temperance — all the fruits of the Spirit — are forces of life. Every one of them is a spiritual force. And every one of them resides in you. You don't have to pray for them, they are already yours. But you do have to tap into them. You have to learn how to exercise them.

Faith, for example, is already yours. You just have to learn to channel it.

There is a scripture with which you are probably already quite familiar. It tells us how this force of faith is developed: **So then faith cometh by hearing, and hearing by the word of God** (Rom. 10:17). According to the Bible, the force of faith is developed and becomes strong and mature by hearing God's Word.

Faith comes by God's Word. Outside of that Word your faith can't be all it was meant to be. If you separate yourself from the Word of God, your faith will never develop as it should.

If that is true of faith, then it could be said: "So then *love, joy, peace, longsuffering, gentleness, goodness, meekness, temperance* cometh by hearing, and hearing by the Word of God." You won't find any verse that uses these words exactly, but the scriptures imply it. Every one of the forces of life is developed the same way — by hearing the Word of God.

The Apostle John says of God: **But whoso keepeth his word, in him verily is the love of God perfected . . . .** (1 John 2:5). The Word of God develops love, and all the other attributes of God's nature, just as it develops faith.

I am convinced that many times we try to center our attention on faith without understanding any of these other forces. It is vitally important that we realize how they are developed, because they are all interdependent. One of them cannot fully function without the support of the others.

For example, if you haven't developed the love of God in your life, then your faith is not going to work too well. The Bible says that **faith...worketh by love** (Gal. 5:6). Now what is going to happen to the person who spends all his time, day in and day out, month after month, trying to develop his faith, if he leaves the love of God lying dormant? He is destined to end up confused and frustrated.

That's the reason so many Christians are constantly struggling with their faith, yet seeming to get nowhere. They know they are supposed to have faith, yet it looks as though despite all their great faith everything in their life is falling apart. They just can't seem to be able to "get a handle" on this faith thing. And they don't understand why not:

"Bless God," they say, "I've been reading all these faith books, and listening to all these faith tapes, but I just can't get my faith to work. I follow all the rules and apply all the principles, but nothing happens. What's wrong? Where am I missing it?"

To those people I would say this: It's fine to want to develop great faith. It's wonderful to saturate yourself with the spoken and written Word of God. There is not a thing wrong with that. But if you don't do something about the parent force of faith — which is love — then your faith is not going to work for you.

In 1 Corinthians 13:2 the Apostle Paul says: **...though I have all faith, so that I could remove mountains, and have not charity** (love)**, I am nothing.** If this was true for Paul, it is certainly true for us. Our faith will not be as effective as it was designed to be, if the love of God is not developed in our life.

There are a lot of people who have got hold of the "you-can-have-what-you-say" message and have gone off the deep end with it. They go around saying everything they know (and a lot they don't). Yet because they are continually in strife, all their "saying" is in vain. They have

29

become as sounding brass, or a tinkling cymbal (1 Cor. 13:1). Yet they cannot understand why they keep saying what they want but it doesn't work.

The answer is simple. The problem is that they have latched onto one aspect of faith — positive confession or affirmation — but have missed the "big picture." They are trying to apply a faith principle without the support of the force of love upon which that principle is based. (It's sort of like trying to climb a ladder with nothing to lean it against — it keeps falling down, and taking them with it.)

It is possible to know all the rules and apply all the right principles, and still not succeed. You can say everything just right, and still fail. Why? Because your confession is empty and idle. Remember: Your saying so doesn't make it so. Confession only works if what you are confessing is true. It is not *your* saying something that makes it true, but the fact that *God* said it first. But if you're going to take a stand on *God's* truth, then you are going to have to make sure you've got the *whole* truth.

In order to reap the benefits of the force of faith — or any other of the forces of life — we must be fully indued with the Spirit of God. And God's Spirit is love. (1 John 4:16.) To have God's power in our mouth and in our hands, we must have His nature in our heart. Without the love of God on the inside, we cannot expect to see the power of God manifested on the outside.

3

The Joy of the Lord

I never realized how powerful joy was until God began to give me this message. He revealed to me that joy is the thrust of faith.

Many Christians are saying things that are not truly faithful confessions because they are not joyful confessions. So many times people confess things out of fear. They confess that something is going to happen because they are afraid it's *not* going to happen. I call that a positive negative.

You can tell by the tone of a person's voice when he is struggling. Although he seems to be saying all the right words, it is evident from his voice and behavior that he doesn't know if his marvelous confession is really working or not. All he knows is that according to what he has heard in church or on T.V., he is supposed to say what he wants. That is not faith, because faith is joyful.

You can tell when you are operating in true faith, because you will have joy rising up out of your spirit. Just as surely as faith is based on love, it is also accompanied by joy. Joy is the thrust behind faith. Without joy, confession is just "wishful speaking."

But if joy is so important to faith, how do we get that joy? Where does it come from? We have learned that faith comes by hearing, and hearing by the Word of God. So does joy.

In the Gospel of John, we have recorded this discourse by Jesus as He was teaching His disciples:

I am the true vine, and my Father is the husbandman. Every branch in me that beareth not fruit he taketh away: and every branch that beareth fruit, he purgeth it, that it may bring forth more fruit.

Now ye are clean through the word which I have spoken unto you.

Abide in me, and I in you.

As the branch cannot bear fruit of itself, except it abide in the vine; no more can ye, except ye abide in me.

34

I am the vine, ye are the branches: He that abideth in me, and I in him, the same bringeth forth much fruit: for without me ye can do nothing.

If a man abide not in me, he is cast forth as a branch, and is withered; and men gather them, and cast them into the fire, and they are burned.

If ye abide in me, and my words abide in you, ye shall ask what ye will, and it shall be done unto you.

Herein is my Father glorified, that ye bear much fruit; so shall ye be my disciples.

As the Father hath loved me, so have I loved you: continue ye in my love.

If ye keep my commandments, ye shall abide in my love; even as I have kept my Father's commandments, and abide in his love.

These things have I spoken unto you, that my joy might remain in you, and that your joy might be full.

John 15:1-11

In this passage, Jesus said that He was saying all these things so that His joy might be in us, and that our joy might be full. (v. 11.) So then, joy comes by hearing our Lord talk. Because what He has to say is good news. That's what the Gospel is, good news. When you hear good news, it ought to create joy on the inside of you.

I can tell you exactly how to determine if what you are hearing at church is the Gospel or false doctrine. If you walk out of there with sorrow or grief or guilt or fear, you were robbed. You should have gone someplace else. You didn't hear the truth — the Gospel truth. But if you walked out of church full of the joy of the Lord, then somebody was preaching the Gospel. Because that's what the Gospel is — *good* news!

Jesus said, "These things I have spoken unto you that your joy might be full." He also said, "If you will listen to Me, you will *remain* full of joy all the time."

When Christians go around sad and grieved, that is a good indication they haven't been listening to God or His Word. They've been listening to something else.

In the next chapter, Jesus told His disciples, **...your joy no man taketh from you** (John 16:22). That's why we are to protect our spirit with all diligence. We are to be careful not to let men take our joy. Why? Because when the world talks, it robs us of joy.

Generally speaking, the world's message and God's message are not the same. When the world speaks, it is not going to agree with God. The world's viewpoint is diametrically opposed to God's viewpoint. The world talks about problems, while God talks about solutions.

In times of economic crisis, inflation, depression, famine, hardship, all the world can give you is bad news. If you lend your ears solely to the world's news, you are bound to end up sad and depressed, because the news media of this world are restricted to reporting what has already happened. Their purpose and duty is to deal with "facts." And much of the time — especially these days — the "facts of life" are negative.

Good News

One time I was in a city where I was holding a series of meetings. One night after church I went back to my hotel and was getting undressed. I had flipped on the television, but wasn't watching it, although I could hear it. The weather report came on, and the weatherman began talking about weather conditions in different parts of the state.

"It's a beautiful day in our city," he said, "but over in the Dallas-Fort Worth area there are severe thunderstorm warnings. It looks pretty bad for those folks over there," he noted, "but, of course, that is Copeland-Savelle country and they won't put up with that sort of thing!"

I thought to myself, "Surely I didn't hear what I thought I just heard."

I had just about convinced myself I had imagined it, when suddenly the telephone rang. It was my associate.

"Did you hear the weather report?" he asked.

"Did that weatherman say what I thought he did?" I responded.

"Yes, he sure did!" my friend confirmed.

So every night after that I could hardly wait to watch the weather report. The weatherman would say things like this: "The national weather bureau is predicting severe weather for up north, but in the name of Jesus Christ of Nazareth, whatever we bind on earth is bound in heaven!"

Needless to say, I liked that weatherman! So I went down to the station to meet him.

"Yes, I am turned on to God," he told me. "I have been reporting the weather on this channel for years. But when I got born again, I began to give the weather report according to the Word of God. The station management has been trying to fire me for a long time now, but the Christians in the viewing area won't let them."

It seems the station had been receiving complaints from people who were saying they didn't want to hear all of that "Jesus stuff" on the weather report. The station director was getting so much flack, he had the weatherman pulled off the air. When the news got around that he had been taken off, the station's telephones wouldn't quit ringing. All of the believers in the area kept calling and demanding that he be put back on, threatening to switch to a different station if he weren't reinstated right away. So the station had no choice but to rehire the man and allow him to give the weather report the way he wanted to.

Now I don't blame the news media for reporting the news in a factual manner. That's their job. It's not their fault that much of what they have to report is negative. That's just the way things are — in the world. ("World News" is a very descriptive title! Except that many times it's more like "World Views." But frankly, I'm really not interested in the world's views, I want to hear God's views!)

I have found that you don't have to depend solely on the media to be fully informed. In fact, if you let the news media be your only source of information, you will soon develop a very unbalanced perspective of what is going on in the world.

It's fine to be informed about local, state, national and international developments. As Christians, I think we should keep abreast of world events. Our

Lord Jesus has commanded us, **Go ye into all the world....** (Mark 16:15a). We are sent out to reap the Lord's harvest. And He has told us, **The field is the world** (Matt. 13:38). Every good farmer knows his field. If he expects to produce a good crop, he must know the condition of his soil.

But while we should know the condition of our field, the world, we should remember that we do not take our solutions *from* the world, we take our solutions *to* the world: **....and preach the gospel** (the Good News) **to every creature** (Mark 16:15b).

The media only reports what is happening; it's not their job to tell us what to do about it. So, I listen to the news. I know what is going on in the world. I just don't let what is happening in the world get me down. I don't let what the world says destroy what my God says. I don't let the world rob me of my joy. Neither should you.

Joy is a force of life. It provides a power to do something about what is going on in the world today. When everything is falling apart all around you, when all the world is weeping and wailing, not knowing which way to turn, in the darkness of despair — that's when you need to stand forth **as a beacon upon the top of a mountain, and as an ensign on a hill** (Is. 30:17). The world may treat you like a fool when things are going good. They may ridicule and reject you in fair weather. But when the storms of life descend upon them like a howling gale, guess who they will turn to for help!

That's why God wants you to be full of joy — for your sake, and for the sake of others. **For the joy of the Lord is your strength** (Neh. 8:10).

4
Count It All Joy

My brethren, count it all joy when ye fall into divers temptations.

Knowing this, that the trying of your faith worketh patience.

James 1:2,3

Anybody can say hallelujah when his needs are all met. Anyone can be happy when everything is going his way. When a person has an abundance of every good thing, it doesn't take much faith at all to say, "Praise God, my needs are met." It does take faith to make that confession when it looks as though he is about to lose it all!

James tells us to count it all joy *when* we fall into divers temptations. That's when we are to be joyful, at the very moment we are beset by temptations, testings and trials. Why then? Because that is when the force of joy is most needed — and most productive.

As Christians we ought to be full of joy all the time. But joy really pays off most when we are under pressure. Because that's when it has the greatest opportunity and challenge to go to work on our behalf.

I heard about a fellow who carries $3,000 around in his pocket all the time. Someone once asked him why he carried so much cash with him. His reply was, "So if I ever need it, I'll have it." That makes sense, doesn't it? That's the only reason any of us ever carry any amount of money — so we'll have it when we need it. That's one of the reasons we need to learn to stay full of joy — so we'll have it when we need it.

That fellow may never need that much money at one time, but if he ever does, it's going to be great to have it. It's also great to know that you have a plentiful supply of joy on hand for any emergency that might present itself in life.

Sooner or later, pressure will come. When people get under pressure, that's when they reveal what they are full of.

Doubt. Unbelief. Anger. Hostility. Resentment. Fear. Whatever a person is full of will be revealed when the pressure comes. That's another reason we need to stay full of the joy of the Lord. To assure that what comes out under pressure is "the right stuff." Without a real sense of joy deep down in our spirit, our faith will not stand up under pressure. Because joy is the thrust of faith. Joy is "faith fuel."

Many people have become dependent upon their faith only to find out that it isn't nearly as developed as they thought it was because they have never developed the other forces of life. That's why their faith confessions fall to the ground right in front of them, because they haven't invested the time and effort necessary to develop the forces that cause faith to work.

The Strength of Combined Forces

Remember that these forces work together. You are never going to get anywhere trying to develop just one force of life. It is impossible to take one force and "super-develop" it. When these forces are working together in harmony, all the demons of hell cannot stop you. When you have all nine of these powerful spiritual forces working for you, it is as though you are surrounded by a protective shield that cannot be penetrated. Not by Satan or his demons. Not by sickness or disease. Not by failure or defeat or anything else. The forces of life build a hedge around you that will repel every attack of the enemy.

If the Church of Jesus Christ could ever release the joy on the inside of each individual believer, nothing would be impossible to us.

Heaven is full of joy and praise. The Bible says that there are thousands upon thousands of angels surrounding the throne of God. Their sole duty and function is to continually cry out: "Holy, Holy, Holy is the Lord God Almighty!" Never in all of history has God ordered that angelic host to hush. God loves praise.

All this continual praise of the Almighty is what irritated the archangel Lucifer so much. He was jealous. He wanted all that praise and glory to go to him, not to God. That's why he led one third of the heavenly host in a rebellion against the Most High. As a result, he and his followers were cast out of heaven and down to the earth where they have been causing trouble ever since.

The fall of man was not the beginning of conflict in the universe — it was only the result of it. The conflict began in the spiritual realm, in heaven. And it began because one creature coveted the praise and glory that rightfully belongs exclusively to the Creator.

So now Lucifer (Satan) plans and plots and schemes against God. Since he cannot attack God directly, he comes against His highest and most cherished creation, man. Satan comes to kill and steal and destroy us because we are made in the image and likeness of our Father. Our adversary does everything he can to wipe us off the face of this planet. Day and night he works to overthrow God by overthrowing us, God's children. Because Satan hates God so much, he hates you and me and everything we stand for. But when he launches his attacks against us, all we have to do is stand firm and shout, *"Hallelujah!"* (Praise the Lord!)

Praise drives Satan up the wall. It immobilizes him. It paralyzes him. It throws him into confusion. That is not the way he wants us to respond. He wants us to cry out in anguish and doubt, "Oh, my God, I can't stand it! Oh, Lord, why is this happening to me?" That is the kind of response our enemy wants from us. Terror. Defeat. Oppression. Depression. He wants to hear us weeping and wailing and crying "bloody murder," because then he has the legal right to commit "bloody murder"!

Satan knows a secret we Christians need to learn. He knows that what we decree with our mouth, we commission to occur. Since we have dominion over the earth, by our negative words we grant our worst enemy the power and authority to bring about our own destruction. That's why what we say is so important. Why we need to control our tongue. As the Word of God warns us: **Death and life are in the power of the**

tongue....(Prov. 18:21). That's also why we need a ready supply of the forces of life — especially the force of joy.

The Bible says to count it all joy *when* we come under pressure. When we Christians finally learn to put our faith where our mouth is and unleash the power that is resident within us, that's when we will begin to cast Satan out of our kingdom just as God cast him out of His!

Laughing in the Face of Defeat

At destruction and famine thou shalt laugh....

Job 5:22

In His Word, God says that we should laugh at destruction and famine. In Psalm 2:4 David wrote: **He that sitteth in the heavens shall laugh: the Lord shall have them** (the heathen) **in derision.**

Why are we Christians so frightened and intimidated by Satan? God certainly isn't. Psalm 37:13 tells us: **The Lord shall laugh at him: for he seeth that his day is coming.**

If God laughs at Satan's puny efforts to dislodge Him from His throne on high, why do we Christians allow the threats and blustering of this defeated foe to create within us an attitude of fear and failure? Especially when we understand that the only way Satan can defeat us is by deceiving or bluffing us into giving him the upper hand by our negative, defeatist words?

God is not affected by the devil's little tricks. Why should we be? Don't we remember that greater is He who is in us than he who is in the world? (1 John 4:4.) God didn't give us that scripture just for a Full-Gospel cliche. That knowledge was not revealed to the Apostle John just so we Christians would have something to sing and confess. God inspired John to make that statement because it is true! Greater is He who is in *you* than he who is in the world! Remember that fact next time you face adversity or trial or tribulation in your life!

Count it all JOY when you fall into divers temptations! As strange as it may seem, as hard as it may be to believe — it *is* a laughing matter! God has said so, and God doesn't lie.

Count it *all* joy. Count *everything* joy, because joy is a force. And it is that force of joy that is your key to victory.

The Power of Praise

Although the fig tree shall not blossom, neither shall fruit be in the vines; the labour of the olive shall fail, and the fields shall yield no meat; the flock shall be cut off from the fold, and there shall be no herd in the stalls:

Yet I will rejoice in the Lord, I will joy in the God of my salvation.

The Lord God is my strength, and he will make my feet like hinds' feet, and he will make me to walk upon mine high places.

Habakkuk 3:17-19

Do you realize what this passage is saying? It is telling us that no matter how desperate the situation may seem, we are to rejoice in the Lord. The Apostle Paul wrote to the Philippians: **Rejoice in the Lord alway: and again I say, Rejoice** (Phil. 4:4). Why? Why should we rejoice when everything seems to be going against us, when there seems no reason at all for joy? The answer is found in the next verse: **...The Lord is at hand** (v. 5).

Despite the circumstances of life, our God has not left us nor forsaken us. He is right there with us, and in us. We have within us the presence and power of Almighty God Himself. Adversity is not the time to surrender, it's the time to draw upon those forces of life within us. It is precisely for moments like this that they were put there!

If we will draw upon those spiritual forces of God within us, the anointing of David will come upon us. David was a man after God's own heart. Do you know why? Because he would shake adversity with a song. That's what the psalms are, praises to God. Forces of joy.

Many times when David was surrounded by his enemies and everything looked totally hopeless, he would lift up his hands and praise God: **...the Lord is the strength of my life; of whom shall I be afraid?** (Ps. 27:1). **The Lord is my strength and song, and is become my salvation** (Ps. 118:14).

In the midst of adversity, David just kept on praising and worshipping God and rejoicing. And God never let him down.

Let the force of joy rise up on the inside of you and give some thrust to your faith. The anointing of the psalmist will come upon you. The anointing of the warrior. God will see you through just as He did David.

In Old Testament days, when God's people came under great attack of the adversary, God did not instruct the king of Israel to assemble his mightiest fighting men, his most skilled warriors. No, He said that He Himself would fight their battles for them. Rather, He ordered that the singers and praisers be sent out in advance of the army. God knew the power of praise.

So should you. When you face adversity, count it all JOY. Then give expression to that joy. You cannot be defeated when the force of joy is being released in your life.

Books by Jerry Savelle

Drawn By His Love
The Life of Holiness

You Can Have Abundant Life

Energizing Your Faith

If Satan Can't Steal Your Joy,
He Can't Keep Your Goods

Victory and Success Are Yours!

Sharing Jesus Effectively

Sowing in Famine

Fruits of Righteousness

God's Provision for Healing

New From Harrison House
The Force of Joy

Available from your local bookstore, or from:

Harrison House
P. O. Box 35035 • Tulsa, OK 74153

Dr. Jerry J. Savelle is a noted author, evangelist, and teacher who travels extensively throughout the United States, Canada, and overseas. He is president of Jerry Savelle Ministries, a ministry of many outreaches devoted to meeting the needs of believers all over the world.

Well-known for his balanced Biblical teaching, Dr. Savelle has conducted seminars, crusades, and convention engagements for a number of years. By the direction of the Holy Spirit, he now holds meetings in local churches and fellowships across the United States. He is being used to help bridge the gap between the traveling ministry and the local church. In these meetings he is able to encourage and assist pastors in perfecting the saints for the work of the ministry. He is in great demand today because of his inspiring message of victory and faith and his accurate and entertaining illustrations from the Bible. He teaches the uncompromising Word of God with a power and an authority that is exciting, but with a love that delivers the message directly to the spirit man.

When Jerry was 12 years old, God spoke to his heart as he was watching the healing ministry of Oral Roberts on television. God told Jerry that He was calling him into the ministry. Some years later, Jerry made Jesus Christ the Lord of his life and since that time has been moving in the light of that calling.

Dr. Savelle is the founder of Overcoming Faith Churches of Kenya, and the missions outreach of his ministry extends to over 27 different countries around the world. His ministry also delivers the powerful message of God's Word to Prison inmates across the United States through the JSM Prison Ministry Outreach.

Dr. Savelle has authored a number of books and has an extensive cassette teaching tape ministry. Nearly 300,000 books and tapes are distributed around the world each year through Jerry Savelle Ministries.

To contact Jerry Savelle,
write:

Jerry Savelle Ministries
P. O. Box 2228
Fort Worth, Texas 76113

*Please include your prayer requests
and comments when you write.*